# A DAY W
# A RIDING INSTF

A DAY IN THE LIFE

# A DAY WITH A RIDING INSTRUCTRESS

Pippa Cuckson and Tim Humphrey

Other titles in this series

Airline Pilot
Ambulanceman
Dancer
Doctor
Farmer
Fireman
Fisherman
Footballer
Lorry Driver
Miner
M.P.
Nurse
Policeman
Publican
Racing Driver
Reporter
Sales Rep
Secretary
Shopkeeper
Soldier
Student
Teacher
Traindriver
T.V. Producer
Vet
Vicar

First published in 1982 by
Wayland Publishers Limited
49 Lansdowne Place, Hove
East Sussex BN3 1HF, England



ISBN 0 85078 282 1

Phototypeset by
Planagraphic Typesetters, London SE1
Printed and bound in Great Britain by
R. J. Acford, Industrial Estate, Chichester, Sussex

# 1. This is Tonia, a riding instructress.

*The British Horse Society awards teaching qualifications to instructors who attain a high standard. If you want to have riding lessons, B.H.S approval is a good thing to look out for when choosing a riding school.*

This is Tonia, who is one of the senior instructresses at Wellington Riding. This is a large and very busy riding centre in Hampshire. Tonia comes from London, but learned to ride at Wellington in her school holidays. She came to work here full-time after getting a degree at Manchester University and has since gained one of the British Horse Society's teaching qualifications.

Tonia thinks she is particularly lucky to work at Wellington.

# 2. Tonia arrives at the stables.

Tonia usually arrives at the stables by 7.00 a.m. Lessons do not usually start until 9.00 a.m., but all the stabled horses have to be fed, groomed, and mucked out beforehand. There are more than fifty stabled horses at Wellington.

Wellington is made up of several small stable yards. This enables the staff to keep the various types of horses together.

There are about a dozen trainees, instructors and grooms at Wellington.

*A competition horse is any horse kept and trained for competitive riding, rather than pleasure riding or school work. Examples of competitive riding are show jumping, horse trials and dressage.*

## 3. She discusses the day's work with Nereide.

Tonia's first task of the day is to plan her timetable with Nereide. Nereide is one of Wellington's owners, and she looks in the diary to see how many lessons have been booked in. The remaining chores will fit in between them.

Tonia will have to take four lessons today, plus a lecture. She must also help the blacksmith, who visits the yard once a week, and exercise Junior, one of the competition horses.

## 4. Tonia pins up the staff rota.

Tonia displays the daily staff rota on the noticeboard. Like her, the other instructors and trainees have already been allocated lessons for the day. They will have to fit their duties in between the lessons.

The noticeboard has many other uses. It carries notices about horse shows which Wellington organizes. Clients can also use the board to advertise secondhand riding clothes, equipment, or anything else they have for sale.

# 5. She looks at the feed chart.

*Despite their large size, horses have delicate digestive systems. A sudden change in their diet could cause a nasty stomach-ache called colic. Colic has to be treated by a vet.*

Tonia is going to prepare the horses' first meal, or 'feed', of the day. First she inspects the feed chart on the wall of the forage store.

Like people, horses have varying tastes and needs. Competition horses have to be kept lean and fit in order to perform well. They eat a lot of high protein food. On the other hand, a pony which is only ridden at weekends or during the holidays, can usually manage on the grass in its field. It would only feed on other food when grass is in short supply.

## 6. Now Tonia makes up a feed.

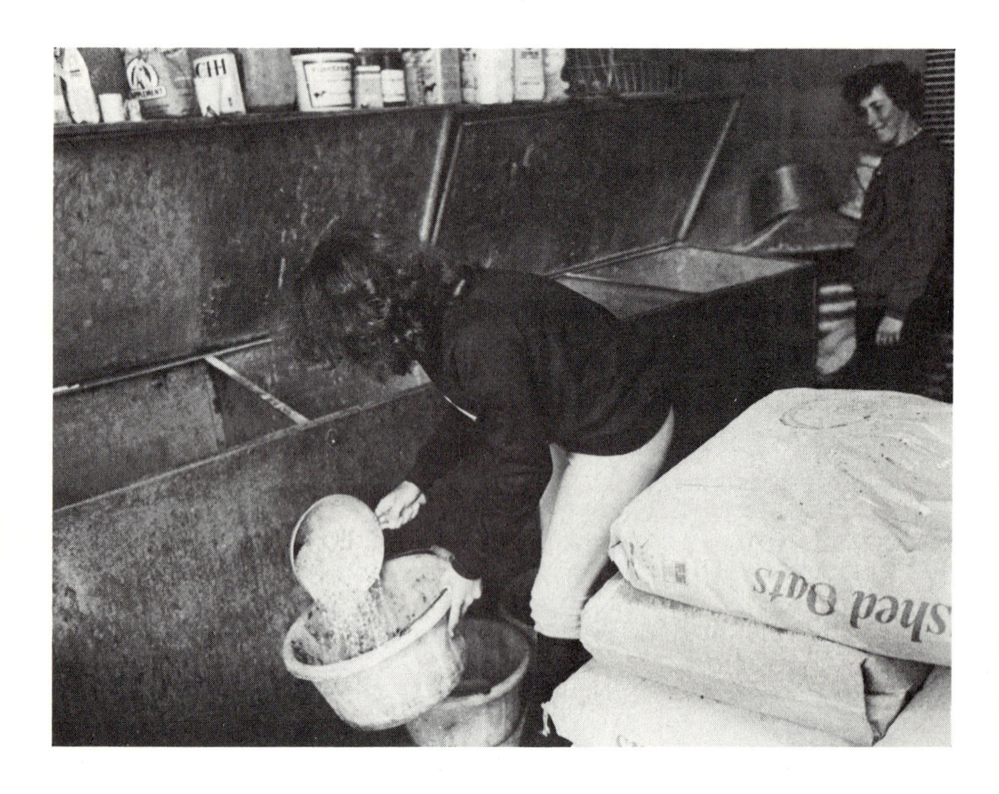

Tonia makes up a feed for Joshua, a competition horse who is staying at Wellington for a week's course with his owner.

She measures out the food in a scoop. Joshua will be having two scoops of oats, one scoop of 'pony nuts', and one scoop of bran. All this is mixed with a 'dollop' of tasty, soaked sugar beet pulp to reduce dustiness.

All the food (oats, barley, nuts and bran) is kept in large, rat-proof metal bins.

*You will see a selection of vitamins and minerals on the shelf, suitable for horses on different diets. Joshua has a measure of one of these, too.*

# 7. Joshua has breakfast.

*All the horses at Wellington have a 24-hour supply of water. Any horse which does not have a regular supply should be offered a drink before its feed. Gulping down a large amount of water* after *a feed is another cause of colic.*

Tonia gives Joshua his early morning feed. She has poured the feed she mixed into his own metal feed bowl. Each horse has his own feed bowl. This reduces the risk of infection if one becomes ill.

Some horses like to play football with their feed bowls! They kick them round the stable, wasting most of their meal. To avoid this problem, some horses have permanent mangers fixed inside the stable, several feet off the ground.

# 8. Tonia collects a shovel.

Tonia is now going to muck out one of the stabled horses in the competition yard. All the mucking out tools — shovels, pitchforks, and rakes — are kept on brackets on the stable wall. It can be very dangerous to leave shovels and forks lying around in the yard.

Tonia selects the tools she needs. Notice the extra-wide yard brooms. There is always a lot of sweeping up to be done.

# 9. She mucks out.

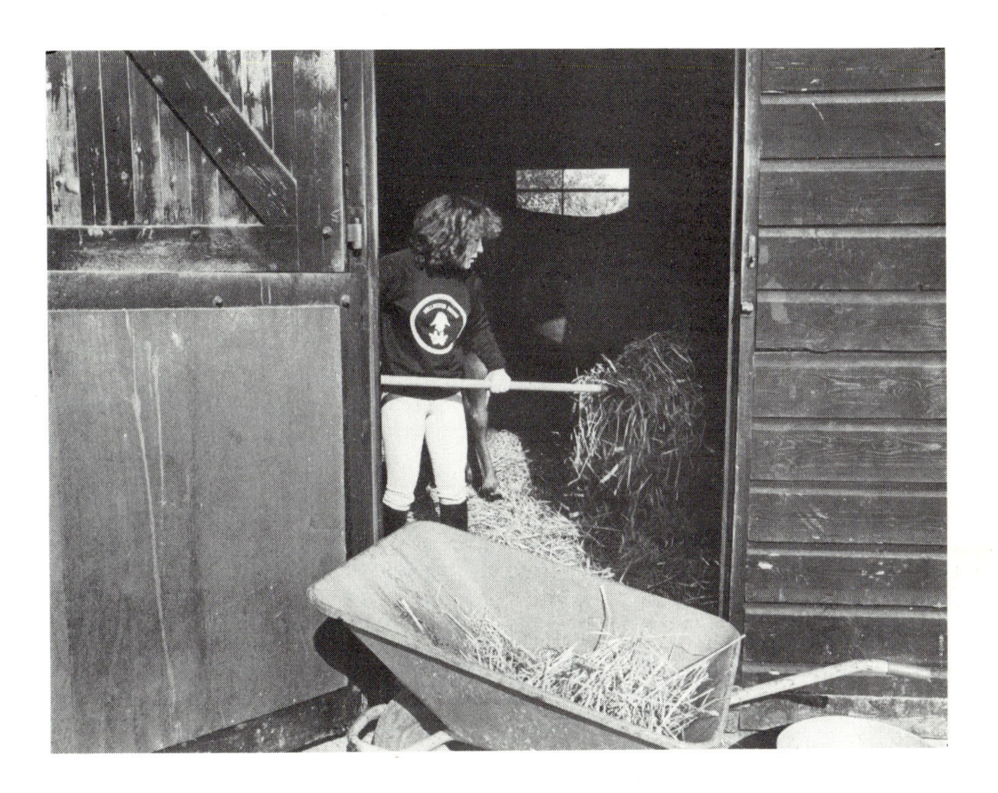

*A horse is said to be 'cast' when he has got wedged against the stable wall after lying down or rolling, and is unable to get up without help.*

Tonia uses the pitchfork and shovel to pick out all the droppings and soiled bedding. She dumps it in the wheelbarrow. Then she tosses up the fresh bedding to make an even layer, and builds up the sides to form 'banks'. These will prevent the horse becoming 'cast'.

This bed is made out of straw. Some horses are bedded down on woodshavings or peat instead, either because they eat the straw, or because it makes them cough.

## **10.** Tonia empties the barrow.

Tonia empties her wheelbarrow on to the muckheap. The straw and manure are allowed to rot down, to make an excellent fertilizer. Many gardeners come to Wellington to buy the manure for their roses.

## **11.** Now she checks the little ponies.

*A pony is a horse which measures 14½ hands or under. A 'hand' is 10 cm (4 in.). The horse is measured to the wither, which is the bony projection at the base of the neck.*

The horses and ponies who live out in the fields are usually brought in to stand in a cool barn during the summer. Then the daytime heat and flies will not irritate them so much. Tonia looks over the ponies to make sure that none of them have cut or bruised themselves during the night.

# 12. Tonia fetches some tack.

Tonia goes into the tack room and collects the saddle and bridle belonging to Viscount. Viscount is the horse which is to be used on her first lesson of the day.

Each horse has his own tack. Horses vary in shape and size, and ill-fitting tack can cause sore backs or mouths.

All the saddles are supported on wooden racks, and the bridles are neatly suspended from hooks on the opposite wall.

*Tack is the collective term for saddles, bridles, and all other equipment used for riding.*

## 13. She takes off Viscount's rugs.

Most of the stabled horses wear a sort of overcoat called a rug at night. This has several purposes. It provides extra warmth; keeps the horse clean; and helps to make a nice shine on the coat.

Many horses who live out wear waterproof 'New Zealand' rugs to keep them warm, dry, and clean in the winter.

## 14. Viscount is groomed.

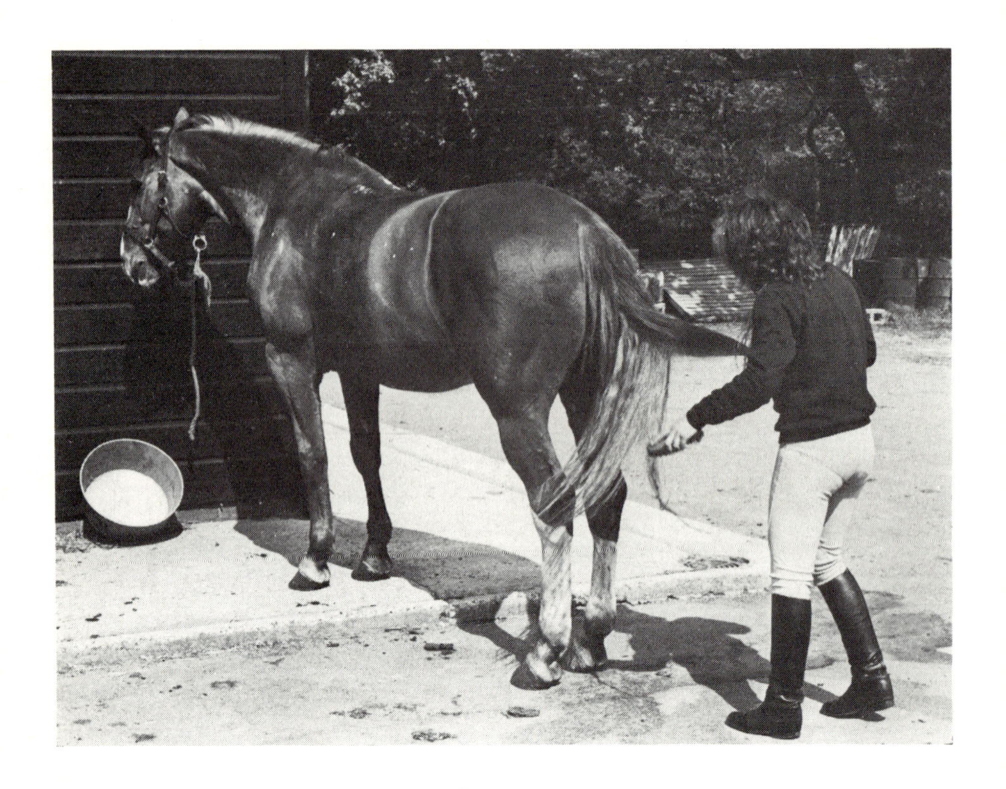

Although Viscount is quite clean, he is groomed every day. A regular brushing helps to tone up the skin and the muscles underneath.

Tonia uses a 'body brush' to groom him from top to toe. She brushes out his mane and tail to remove bits of bedding, and improve his appearance. She may clean the body brush with a metal 'curry comb'. Another type of brush often used is a stiff-bristled 'dandy brush' which removes dried mud.

## **15.** Tonia puts on his saddle.

*The pommel is the front of the saddle. The cantle is the rear of the saddle. The gullet is the channel which runs between them, clearing the horse's spine.*

Tonia puts Viscount's saddle on. She does this by placing it on his neck, and then sliding it down till it reaches a natural resting place. She makes sure that the saddle does not press on Viscount's spine. It should be supported by the muscles on either side, and she should be able to see daylight all along the gullet from cantle to pommel.

Tonia then secures the girth — the strap which keeps the saddle on.

## **16.** Tonia puts on Viscount's bridle.

Tonia pops her thumb into the corner of Viscount's mouth — where no horse has any teeth — and encourages him to open it. Then, in the same movement, she eases the bit into his mouth. She will then be able to slip the top of the bridle over his ears, and secure the buckles.

There are hundreds of different bits. Viscount wears a fairly common, jointed steel bit called a snaffle. It is an 'eggbutt' snaffle — a snaffle with rings at the sides which are fixed, not loose.

## 17. Viscount sets off for his first lesson.

Tonia leads Viscount out to have his lesson. He is to be used to give a 'lunge' lesson to Debbie, Joshua's owner. This means that Tonia will control him with a long 'lunge rein', leaving Debbie to concentrate on her riding. You will notice that Viscount also wears a type of bitless bridle. This is a lunging cavesson, to which the lunge rein will be attached.

Tonia has smartened herself up for the lesson. Around the yard the staff usually wear sweatshirts. For lessons they put on a shirt and tie.

## **18.** Debbie loosens up.

Debbie is staying at Wellington for a week's refresher course. She has found that she sits rather too stiffly in the saddle.

Tonia gives her some exercises on the lunge to loosen up. Debbie is confident to carry them out because she knows Tonia has control of the horse. Tonia asks her to sit up tall and drop her arms to her sides.

## 19. More exercises.

Tonia commands Viscount to trot on in a circle. She gets Debbie to relax, and then stretch out her arms and twist from side to side. This will loosen her shoulders, back and hips.

Lunging is a way of training both horses and riders. If you have ever given someone a piggy-back, you will know how difficult it is to move if they keep shifting their weight from side to side, or bump up and down. It is the same for the horse. The sooner Debbie improves her 'seat', the better Joshua will go.

## 20. The telephone rings.

Debbie's lesson is over, and the next class has not yet begun. Tonia takes her turn answering the telephone.

Wellington receives many telephone calls. People want details about lessons, forthcoming shows, horses for sale, and just general advice.

This caller wants to book a series of lessons during the school holidays. Tonia writes them down in the diary.

## 21. Tonia checks a young rider's tack.

*Wellington insists that everyone wears a hard hat at all times when mounted. Anyone who rides without a hard hat is extremely foolish. Accidents happen when you least expect them and you can be very seriously injured if you land on your unprotected head.*

The next lesson is for a group of children on their school holidays. Most of them have had a few lessons, and are good enough to manage the ponies without help.

Each child is encouraged to tack-up the pony he or she is to ride that day. Tonia inspects their efforts, and shows them where they have gone wrong. She also makes sure they are wearing a hard hat.

## **22.** Tonia helps her pupil to mount.

Tonia holds on to the pony while his rider mounts. The girl has slipped her left foot into the stirrup, and grasped the far side of the saddle. Now she will pass her right leg gently over the pony's back to avoid alarming him, and carefully sit down.

## 23. Then she adjusts the stirrups.

Tonia makes sure the rider is comfortable, and helps her adjust the stirrups to a suitable length.

She will then tighten the pony's girth. Many horses cleverly 'blow out' their stomachs when the rider tightens the girth, so that it is loose when they breathe out. Riders have to catch them unawares, and check the girth when mounted.

## 24. The class sets off for the lesson.

Tonia is taking the class to the sand arena down the lane. Wellington has the use of several different types of riding surface — grass, wood-shavings, and sand — and Tonia has chosen the sand today because it remains soft in hot, dry weather.

One of the junior instructors has come along to assist her with this lesson.

## 25. The rides start with exercises.

The class walks round the arena in single file. Before the riders start proper work, Tonia makes them carry out some exercises. These exercises help to develop an 'independent seat' — this means the ability to sit firmly in the saddle without relying on the reins. The reins are there only to give gentle signals, not to hang on with!

## **26.** Each of the riders trots.

Tonia is teaching the riders to trot today. She explains that the pony will shorten his frame when he trots, and that the rider must therefore shorten the reins to keep in contact with the mouth. The rider then squeezes the pony's sides with his legs, which tells the pony to trot.

The riders learn to rise out of the saddle and sit again in time with the rhythm of the trot, which is more comfortable for them both.

# 27. Tonia greets the farrier.

Tonia's next task is to help Clive, the farrier. Farriers are people who shoe horses; they are usually blacksmiths. Very few blacksmiths have village forges today. Instead, like Clive, they travel to their clients.

Clive visits Wellington once a week and expects to re-shoe about eight or nine horses today. He has brought some ready-made shoes with him.

## 28. Clive trims a hoof.

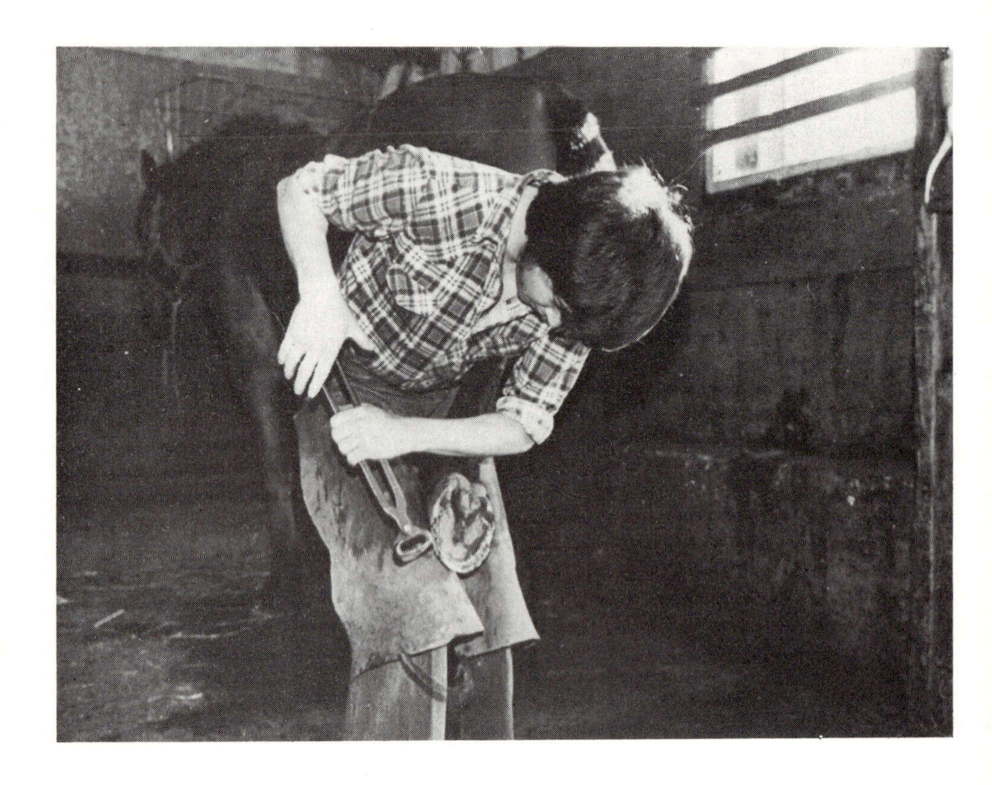

First, Clive removes the old, worn shoes from the pony's feet. He then trims the hoof to correct the shape and provide a level surface for the new shoe.

The wall of a horse's foot is like our fingernails — it has no feeling, but is growing all the time. The hooves must be trimmed regularly, usually every four to six weeks.

Some of the ponies at Wellington are not shod. This is because they do very little work and move only on a soft surface.

## 29. Then he knocks the shoes into shape.

Clive takes a set of ready-made horseshoes and alters them to fit the horse's hooves exactly. He uses a portable furnace to heat the shoes until they are red-hot, and then shapes them with a hammer on an anvil. Finally he will punch about seven holes into each shoe to take the nails.

# 30. Clive nails on the shoes.

Clive nails the shoe to the hoof. This does not hurt the horse, as the nails go through the 'dead' part of the hoof.

Farriers need a lot of knowledge and skill, for bad shoeing can cripple a horse. All farriers have to spend several years apprenticed to a qualified blacksmith, and pass strict examinations before they can set up a business on their own.

Clive tidies up the newly shod hoof by clipping off the ends of the nails, and filing off the rough edges.

## 31. Tonia gives a lecture.

Every day the instructors have a half-hour lecture from senior members of staff. Today's topic is road safety.

There are over two million regular horse riders in Britain. Sadly, there are eight accidents every day involving horses.

Horses are very nervous and are easily startled. Car drivers should give horses a wide berth, pass slowly, and not rev the engine or hoot.

Tonia suggests that riders should encourage good driving by thanking drivers with a wave.

## 32. The horses have their lunchtime water.

It is time for lunch, so most of the stabled horses have another feed. Tonia is topping up their water buckets.

Behind her, two of the instructors are sweeping up for the second time that day. The yard is continually littered with mud, hay and straw.

## **33.** Tonia ties up a hay net.

Most of the horses have some hay at lunchtime. It is put in a giant string bag called a hay net, and tied to the wall. This stops the horse from trampling it into the bedding.

Some very old stables have hay racks fixed high on the walls. This sort of rack is not used often today, as the seeds and dust tend to fall into the horse's eyes and ears, and cause irritation and infection.

# **34.** Tonia lunches at the pub.

Tonia and the other senior members of staff are taking a break from the stables during the lunch hour. Today Tonia, Nereide, and Maxine have gone to the pub for an hour.

The junior and student instructors live in a hostel near the stables and have lunch there.

## 35. A lesson in the indoor school.

The first lesson of the afternoon is in the indoor school. Tonia is supervising two of the junior instructors and Debbie on Joshua.

Today many large riding centres have indoor schools. This enables them to give lessons in all weathers and also at night time, using artificial light.

## **36.** Tonia rides Joshua.

Debbie has found that Joshua, like many horses, is stiffer on the left side than he is on the right. Tonia rides him for a few minutes to see for herself. Tonia and Debbie then discuss ways of making Joshua more supple. Tonia suggests that Debbie should ride a series of circles and turns to the left to make Joshua work his lazy, stiff muscles.

## **37.** She treats a sore leg.

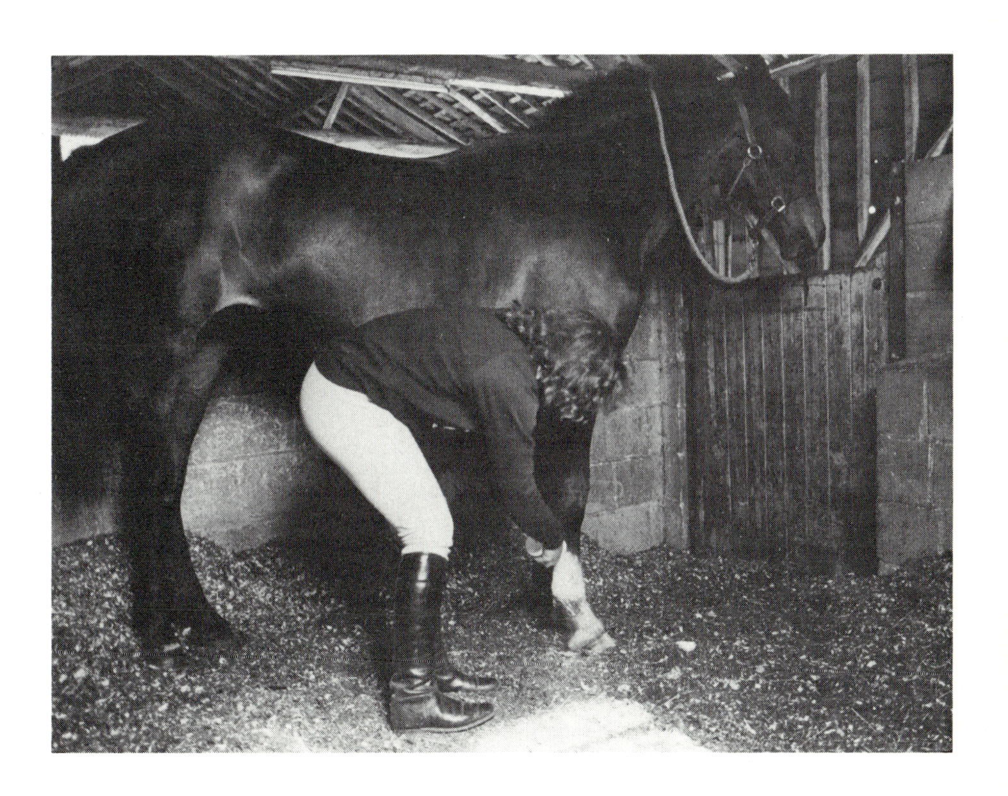

This horse is Wellington Vittoria, the Irish mare Tonia rode at the Badminton Horse Trials this year.

Unfortunately, 'Vit' hurt her leg some months ago, and recently had an operation to put it right. She still needs special care. Tonia has been given some soothing powder by the vet, and is sprinkling it on Vit's leg.

## **38.** Tonia mounts Casterbridge.

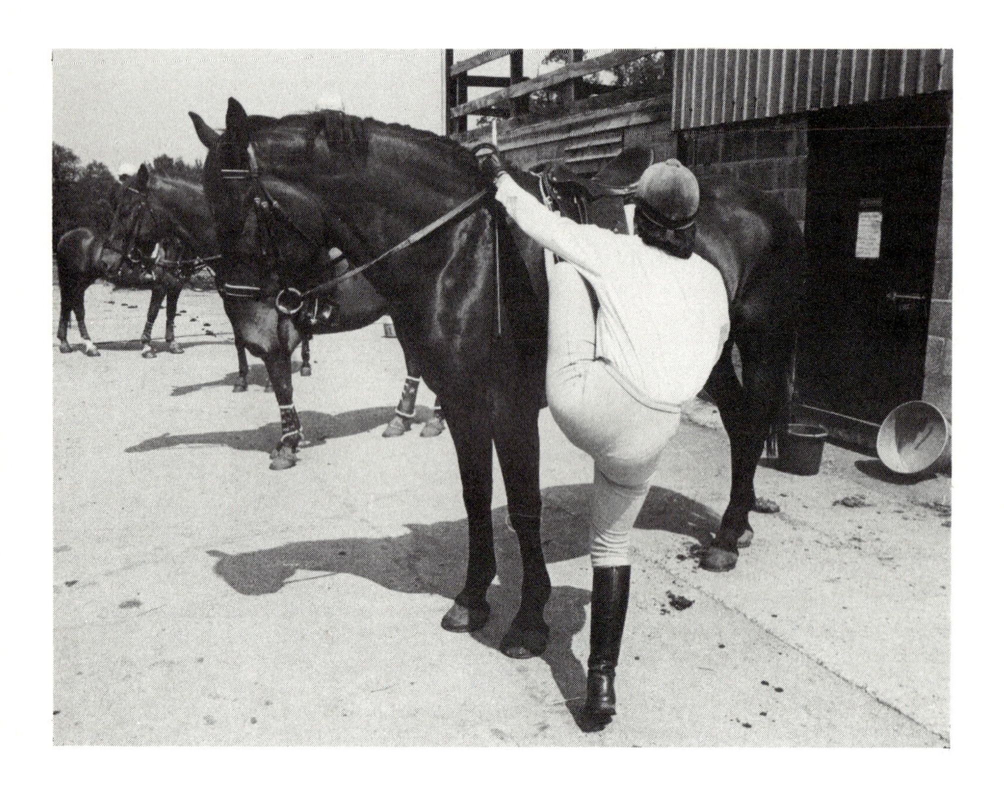

Tonia is now going to give a cross-country jumping lesson. The fences are spread all over the eighty acres surrounding the main yard. It is too far for her to walk, so she is going to ride Casterbridge. He is one of the liveries, and needs the exercise.

*A livery is a privately owned horse which is stabled and cared for by Wellington Riding for a fee. The horse's owner is too busy to look after his horse properly, or he does not have space.*

## **39.** Tonia explains the cross-country lesson.

Tonia lines up her three pupils and tells them what they are going to learn today.

You will notice that the three riders have all put on extra strong jockey or 'skull' caps, with a padded strap under the chin. This is because cross-country riding can be hazardous. Special care has to be taken. The horses wear special protector boots on their legs to prevent them from knocking themselves.

## **40.** Debbie jumps a log.

First to go, Debbie and Joshua tackle a large log. They clear it quite well, although Tonia notes that Joshua got too close before he took off and therefore jumped in a rather awkward fashion.

She will tell Debbie to jump it again and see if the horse will jump better.

## 41. Denise jumps down the steps.

Denise, who is riding Rosie, jumps down the 'steps'. When jumped this way the obstacle forms a 'drop' fence – a fence with a drop on the far side. Rosie might suddenly stretch her neck down if she needs to balance herself. Therefore Denise sits up quite tall and is ready to let the reins slip through her fingers.

## 42. Back at the stables Joshua has a bath.

Tonia and Debbie decide to give Joshua a bath to help him cool off. He has worked hard today, and the weather has been hot and sticky.

Tonia holds him while Debbie wets him with water from a hose-pipe, and sponges him down with some 'horse shampoo'. She will then put on his anti-sweat rug – a type of string vest for horses. This will help him dry off.

*Most horses enjoy a bath, but summer is the only time they should have one. They could get cold and catch a chill if bathed in winter. Detergent and water removes the grease from their coats which helps to keep them warm and healthy.*

## 43. Tonia takes a tea break.

Tonia's chores are nearly over for the day. She takes a tea-break with Maggie who manages the office.

Maggie adds up the takings for the day, and makes sure that they tally with the bookings in the diary. She is pleased to note another profitable day. All the horses – and instructors – have earned their keep!

**44.** Tonia reads a magazine.

Tonia and Debbie glance through copies of the equestrian magazines which have arrived at Wellington.

They are interested to find a large picture of one of Tonia's eventing friends. Perhaps Tonia and Vit may find themselves in there one day.

This is the first real chance Tonia has had to relax all day, apart from the lunch-break. Teaching has finished, but there is still a lot of work to be done.

*Equestrianism means the skill and the art of good horse riding.*

*Eventing is a type of competition which tests the all-round ability of a horse and rider. It is made up of dressage, cross-country and show-jumping.*

# **45.** Now it is time to ride Junior.

*The Badminton Three-Day Event is one of the best known equestrian competitions in Britain.*

Tonia rides Wellington Junior, one of the competition horses in her charge.

Junior is six years old and has just won his first novice horse trials. Tonia hopes one day to ride him at Badminton.

'Little, but often' is the schedule of Junior's training. He has about twenty minutes concentrated schooling every day. You might notice how elegantly he carries himself compared with some of the other horses pictured in this book.

## 46. Tonia finishes with some jumps.

Tonia ends Junior's lesson with some jumping. Junior enjoys his jumping, as you can probably see from his happy expression and pricked up ears. Letting him 'pop' a few fences is Tonia's way of saying 'thank you' for working well. She is looking forward to his next attempt at a horse trial.

## 47. Then she puts Junior to bed.

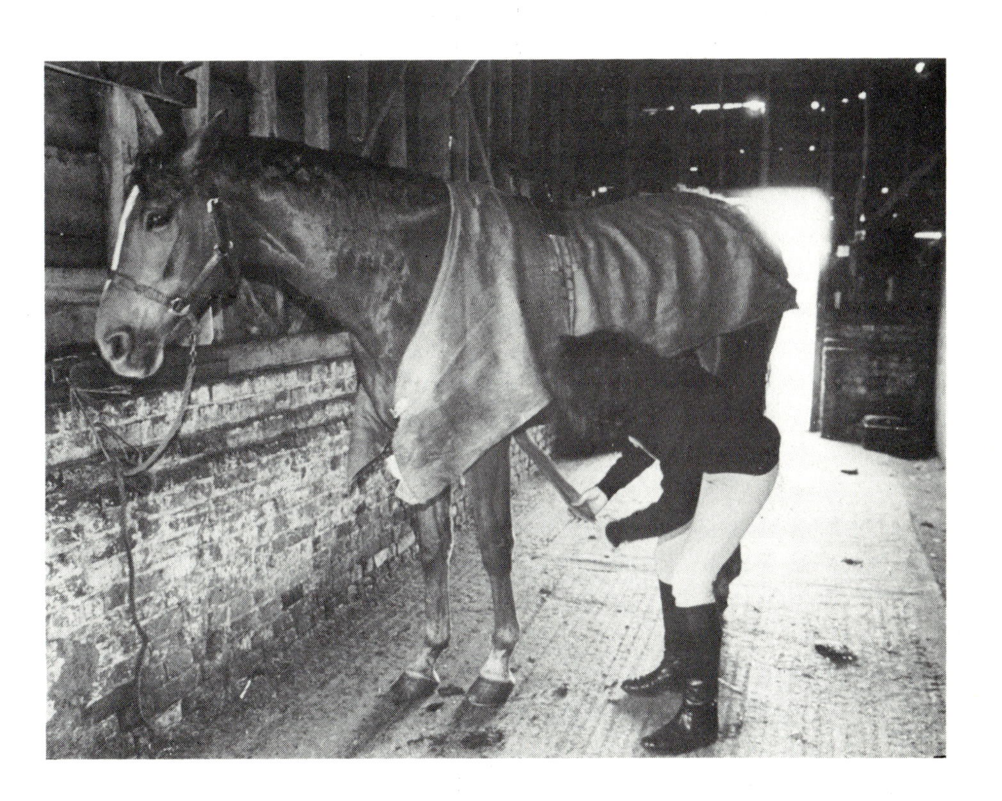

Tonia takes off Junior's tack and rugs him up for the night. Junior's night rug is made out of jute lined with wool. It is fastened with a buckle at the front. Junior also wears a type of belt called a roller round his body. This is a wide strap with padding where it crosses the spine to avoid soreness and pressure.

## **48.** Tonia checks over the stables.

Tonia looks round her yard to make sure that all the horses have plenty of hay and water for the night. All the stables are being mucked out again, and once more the yard is swept.

She makes sure that all the horses are rugged up, and that no one has left any tools or pieces of equipment in the stables which could injure the horses during the night. Finally she ensures that all the doors are properly secured.

## 49. She puts out some hay.

Some ponies which normally live out at grass cannot cope with all the rich grass which grows in the spring. They eat too much of it, and can suffer from a very unpleasant condition called laminitis, which causes inflammation of the feet. Ponies prone to this complaint are kept on a sand-patch for this part of the year. Here their diet can be controlled. Tonia is giving one of these ponies his daily ration of hay.

## **50.** The horses have their own evening meal.

Finally, Tonia gives the last 'hard' feed of the day to the competition horses. As you can see, they are pleased to see her! This will be the last feed of the day for most of them. However, some of the horses which are working extra hard will be given a late night feed. Members of staff take turns to look over the stables around 10 p.m. each night.

## 51. Tonia leaves for home.

Tonia, Maxine, and Nereide are the last to leave. They check that all is in order, lock up the office and tack rooms, and set the burglar alarm.

Tonia is glad it is not her turn to do late night stable duty.

She has worked solidly for over eleven hours. There is nothing like a combination of exercise, fresh air, hot weather, and a long day to make you feel tired.

## 52. Tonia arrives home.

Tonia arrives home at 7 p.m. She used to live in the staff hostel but now shares a house in a nearby village with Maxine. Although devoted to horses, they both like to get away from the stable environment at the end of the day.

Tonia is looking forward to changing out of her grubby clothes. Breeches and shirts may be smart but they pick up a lot of dirt!

## **53.** She helps prepare the supper.

Tonia and Maxine take turns to prepare the evening meal. Tonight it's Tonia's turn, and she is making spaghetti bolognese. They want something quick, filling and easy to prepare. Both are looking forward to putting their feet up and having a television supper.

## **54.** The end of a long, hard day.

Tonia and Maxine often spend the evenings in the pub with friends, or at the pictures, or at parties. Today, however, was tiring, and tomorrow looks even busier. Therefore they both want an early night.

With her good education, Tonia could easily find a less tiring job. She has firmly decided, however, that office life is not for her. She will choose outdoor life with horses any day.

## Books to read

If you would like to learn more about riding and working with horses, the following books should be of interest:

*A Guide to Careers with Horses* by Valerie Russell (Pelham Horsemaster Series).

*An Illustrated Guide to Horse and Pony Care* compiled by Jane Kidd (Salamander Books).

*The Instructors Handbook of the British Horse Society and the Pony Club* (British Horse Society).

*The Manual of Horsemanship of the British Horse Society and the Pony Club* (Country Life Books).

*Training for a Career with Horses* (British Horse Society).

The address of the British Horse Society is British Equestrian Centre, Stoneleigh, Kenilworth, Warwickshire.

The authors wish to thank

Antonia Gray

John and Nereide Goodman, Maxine Cave,
and the staff and pupils
of Wellington Riding

Clive Duffin